Visioning Board Secrets

An Easy Step-by-Step Guide of how to Create a
Vision Board and Host Vision Board Parties -
Vision Board Party 101

Kimberly Millionaire

Visioning Board Secrets

An Easy Step-by-Step Guide of how to Create a Vision Board and Host Vision Board Parties - Vision Board Party 101

DEDICATION

To everyone fiercely pursuing their dreams.

I once heard Myles Munroe say something like:

"The proof of desire is in the pursuit."

Facts.

So keep going.

ACKNOWLEDGMENTS

God. All by Himself.

Visioning Board Secrets

An Easy Step-by-Step Guide of how to Create a Vision Board and Host Vision Board Parties - Vision Board Party 101

VISION BOARD SECRETS

The art of visualization has been around for thousands of years. The Roman emperor, Marcus Aurelius was a stoic or negative visualizer. In this regards, he visualized what might go wrong with a plan and then formatted ways to overcome the negative obstacle he came up with.

In modern times, the practice of visualization was made famous by authors like Wallace D. Wattle. He wrote a book in 1910. This has become a classic in the self-development field, and many of the books written recently about visualization got their start from "The Science of Getting Rich." Wallace Wattles was ahead of his time in using the idea of creative visualization to accumulate wealth amongst other things.

Another well-known book in this area is "As a Man Thinketh," by James Allen. James Allen used a bible passage as his title for the book, hence the word... "Thinketh." The idea of his book basically states "you are what you think about and what is in your heart." His idea was, if you have bad intentions in your heart, you will not be able to attract good things into your life.

Both books are classics and still, widely read today. Many people including famous musicians have stated how these books helped them create a new healthy mind and body. Since both books have been in the public domain for many years, many people have used the books to create not only a better life but a thriving business as well.

Books and other items that are no longer under copyright due to the age can be used to add to or create a "work at home business." This business model was adopted by Matt Furey with massive success. The backbone of his business was built on using public domain books in both self-development and martial arts. While you may not be interested in creating a company from such books, they can be beneficial to read and then use some of the concepts to build your vision boards.

In this eBook, we will be covering the 'Vision Board,' a fantastic tool that can be used for any area of your life.

Take the 10-Day Vision Board Challenge! – https://kimberlythemillionaire.thinkific.com/courses/10-day-visioning-board-challenge

What Exactly is a Vision Board?

A vision board is typically a picture/word board made with the poster boards you can purchase at many stores in the office supplies or stores like Walmart. We generally say you would make this type of purchase because that is the first type of vision board that was used by entrepreneurs. Then it was expanded, and digital vision boards became popular as well.

Vision boards are a huge part of the Law of Attraction, which has become very popular over the years. Making and creating in the LOA idea is making it known to the universe, what you want and in turn, the world works to make this come true. You do not have to believe in the Law of Attraction idea. You do need to believe that when you write down, create images and think with laser focus, about want you want to create for your life...you will make it come true.

A physical vision board that is placed over your desk will contain images that invoke powerful positive thoughts. The photos that you search for, then transfer to your board, will match the written words that are placed around the images. The images that you find in magazines or books should be bright and positive. Many people use colored pencils to add in the written words. The color will help you to focus on the images and words. There is no limit to what you can use to write with, just choose what inspires you.

How Does it Work?

How many random thoughts go through your mind in one day? Have you ever sat down and considered that? Take a moment now and do a quick calculation. The most likely answer that will pop into your mind is that there are far too many thoughts in a jumbled mess and you cannot correctly count them. Just to illustrate that, consider the idea once proposed that said, men think about sex every seven seconds. There is no research to back that statement up. Yet if we are truthfully, then we know that men and women think about sex frequently throughout the day. Add in all the other thoughts about family, money, and work...then we can be sure most of us have unfocused minds.

A vision board helps to quiet that mind and bring clarity to what we truly want in life. Vision boards also help us to focus on making our desires come true. With a vision board, we can write our most powerful affirmations, to signal our brains that this is what we want to come true. Let's expand on this thought even further. We know that we need clarity in our life if we are going to succeed. A vision board helps us to gain clarity by finding images that match exactly what our desires are. When we put a board together, we spend time searching for an image that we need, which means we will disregard a lot of pictures because they are not an exact match. Once we find what we need, it is put on the board, and then we need to match words with the image that invoke strong feelings.

A vision board helps us to focus in several ways. Physically, the board we build will be about the size of a big screen television.

The field of focus, when we look at our board is narrowed. Our eyes are glued to what we have created, rather than looking around our workspace for inspiration. Due to the laser focus with our eyes, we then begin to really focus on what we need to do, to get what we want.

The Power of a Vision Board: What Champions and High Performers Do

Using a vision board helps to create champions and peak performance. Champion athletes often write out their goals as a list on the board and then find images to support those goals.

They often find that while they are right in the middle of needing great motivation, they may not be able to recall a particular written goal; however, the image they chose will shine brightly in their mind.

When observing some athletes before a pole vault or a ski run, it may be noted that they are in the "zone." This means that what they have visualized upon their vision board is now being accomplished right at that moment. Some athletes will start to make the motion of running, jumping or paddling to the point that their body believes they are actually performing.

Their intensity may be such, that their eyes roll back a bit in their head. In neuro-linguistic programming, known in short form as NLP-the idea of eye movement hard to the left, right or even upwards, means the eye muscle is activating different portions of the brain. We need to remember something, for instance, it is believed when you are asked, "how are you feeling?" you will look down and to the right, to access an answer that matches your emotion. "I am feeling sad, or I am feeling depressed," would be a typical response. Eye movement in sports performance is something that most people do not think about. It will be the same when you start to picture thoughts in your head, in regards to creating your vision board.

High performers that create and use vision boards, in a sense are creating an ignition key, ready to fire up the brain for peak performance.

The Benefits of Creative Vision

Having a vision board will help put it all together for you; your goals, your motivation and much more is tied into your journals, written goals and of course the vision board.

There are benefits to using creative vision. Before you can create a vision board that will serve you, it is essential to know how you feel about the elements you want on your board. If you put down on your board a picture of a beautiful house, but it doesn't move you, then you need to discard that.

Try sitting quietly in a comfortable chair. Clear your mind and then think about creating the perfect house. What emotions do you feel? Do you feel ecstatic, negative or just plain neutral? The benefit of using creative vision helps to weed out what you don't want and bring forth what truly matters to you.

Perfecting what you want, will occur when you use creative vision. You will see your vision in your mind and play with it. Alter it or tweak it as you see fit. Add colors, shapes, and sounds. Think of it like this; if you want a sports car, and you just picture a sports car, what sort of emotion will you feel towards it? You have the privilege of making that sports car come alive in your mind by making as many creative changes as you want. What color will the car be, will there be add-ons both inside and out? How will the interior smell? When you do this, you will come up with exactly what you want, and your brain will start to search for ways to make it happen.

Having a creative vision will give you the benefit of working on every area in your mind, deleting what is not needed and adding what you need to do to achieve it. You can use your creative vision on your relationships, finances, work and your spirituality just to name a few.

The Science Behind Vision Boards

When you see a tennis player bouncing the ball in one set motion, over and over, perhaps you are wondering what are they doing? As the tennis player is getting set to serve, they want to get into what they call the "zone."

What they are really doing, is activating an area in their brain, that has been programmed to respond with an affirmative action. The neurons in the tennis players' brain have created what is called pathways. The first time the tennis player bounced the ball in that way to get into the zone of making an ace, a path was built from one neuron to another. The more the same action was repeated, the stronger that pathway becomes. It is like forging a samurai sword, where metal is bent and repeatedly folded until the sword is virtually unbreakable.

Science has looked into the process of creating positive habits and actions. They discovered how repeating a positive action whether in your mind or physically... produces the same results.

When the brain sees the action being done, over and over, it believes what it sees and works on making it a reality.

The book we spoke of before, "The Science of Getting Rich" by Wallace Wattles, talks about the idea of what we pay the most attention to and then taking action on that.

By doing research, scientists now understand that we have a portion of the brain that acts as a receiver. They call this small spot, the reticular activating system. This spot in the brain picks up the information that is fed to the brain. It acts as a filter, discarding what is unimportant and sending on the information it believes the brain needs. It can flag information it deems as very important and then gives you an alert.

Here is a graphic example. Most people have heard the sound of a shotgun being pumped for firing. That sound is terrifying, and it is very likely that your reticular activating system, "RAS" for short - has stored that as very important and gives your brain an alert if heard. Your instant reaction would have your fight or flight response activated...adrenaline is now pumping to provide you with energy to run and duck.

Vision boards will help your RAS, to create alerts and grab hold information that is relevant to your goals. The RAS has been tuned for a particular frequency and when a signal appears and even a weak one, it will start fine-tuning until it is centered and receiving 100%.

The Top 3 Reasons You Need A Vision Board Now

1. Have you ever self-sabotaged yourself or became totally stuck? You cannot move forward, and you are basically running in place. It is incredibly frustrating and often leads to depression.

   When you are unhappy, all your relationships suffer. Put an end to self-sabotage and depression by taking massive action right now. Get out of neutral and start living the life you deserve. Building a vision board gives you a totally fresh start. You get to re-image the life you want and deserve.

   By placing the right images and text for you on the vision board, you tell the universe what you will have in your life. There is now a clear path with action steps, and you have clarified what you will become as if it has already happened.

2. Sometimes you go into neutral or even total reverse if you don't fix your situation. You can find yourself in an infinite loop of getting up, eating just to fill your stomach.

   Many people clock watch as they go through the motions of getting ready to go to work. They start thinking of how to call in sick at the last moment. It's a mental fight, then they shrug and head off to jobs they hate. After clocking in and filling time, it's off to home. Just like washing dirty clothes they rinse and repeat. You're stuck and feeling down, or you have shifted into neutral, were nothing really registers in your mind.

Building a vision board will electrically charge your positive emotions. Everyone needs to be fully alive and awake, to experience all that life has to offer. Everyone needs vision boards in their life.

3. Being pulled in many directions, you sometimes lose focus on what is really important. Everyone has obligations, and some have major ones that they have difficulty fulfilling. It seems like there is smog hanging over their heads every day, and they cannot see beyond the negativity.

    Having a vision board gives you a daily reminder of who you are now and who you are becoming. You need a guidance system just like a jet that is flying from North America to Europe. Step by step, day by day, you build the habit of creating the life you desire, and there is no mystery as to what is going to happen. You develop a clear vision, on that, you can see with great focus.

Vision board experts look at their boards repeatedly throughout the days to stay on track and be totally clear on what is truly important to them.

Vision Board vs. Dream Board

Frequently you will see people referring to a vision board and a dream board as being the same thing. They are actually different and should be used hand in hand. The best way to achieve goals is to break your goals down into 90 days, rather than for a year. The idea is the same with vision vs. dream.

Vision boards should be about what will happen in the short term. This is where you learn to connect with yourself and the universe. In building a vision board, you look for images and phrases, which represent what you need in your life right now to take you to the next level. When we talk about putting a picture of a house on the vision board, this should be the house you need at the moment...a house that serves your needs. A dream board house would be the house you need in the later phase of life... with all the comforts you ever desired.

You want to find images and wording that will activate your RAS and start high powered visualization to take action on. The sooner that you can use the science of attraction, the faster you will build the foundation. The dream board goes on top of the foundation you just created.

The dream board is the items you wanted in your life and perhaps didn't have the courage or financial background to attain yet. Think bucket goals like climbing Mount Everest which requires massive planning and training or achieving success to the point that you can take two months off and travel all of South America.

Turning Your Vision Board Into an Action Board

Once your vision board is complete, realize you are not done. Yes, you will be sitting in front of the board, looking at what you have created and implanting those thoughts in your mind... to be worked on. However, we need also to take action.

Massive action will propel your vision. You need to take the items on your vision board and create an action board. This board will have the lists you need to get into action. Put down what thing you want to work on from your vision board and then the action steps required to do it now.

For example, on your vision board, you might have a picture of a person sitting behind a large office desk and wrote in, "General Manager." This might mean you are now a team leader or supervisor in your organization. Yet you know that becoming General Manager is a position you highly desire and you have a few things noted as to why that is so.

On your action board, you would continue with the General Manager theme and write down the steps you need to take now to accomplish that.

Also, write down the exact time and date you will do those steps and when you expect that those steps will put you into the General Managers chair.

Getting yourself into action may require you to find a way to hold yourself accountable or have an accountability partner.

Align with your values. In the case of becoming the General Manager, ask yourself will you need to do something that is against your values? Doing a short cut, that may impact another person negatively, would for most people-cause the final outcome to be tainted. Stay positive in your mindset and your actions while preparing both the boards for vision and action.

Vision Boards Can Work in Every Area of Your Life

- **Business** - Vision boards can and should be used for any type of business. It doesn't matter if you're a sole proprietor or an employee of a large organization, vision boards help to focus on goals and gain clarity as to what you want to attract to your business. More clients, money and of course continued growth. The ability to create a vision board and share it with friends, family, co-workers and like-minded communities... means you get plenty of feedback. With feedback, you can adjust and tweak your board from time to time and make significant growth.

- **Wealth** is something that the vast majority of people want. Yet it is best to remember that attracting wealth through a vision board takes some serious thought. Gaining wealth and then hoarding it, will not bring happiness.

The real purpose of a vision board is to be well rounded. When creating a vision board about wealth, spend time thinking about what you will do when the money begins to appear. Will you share it with family and friends? Will you do good deeds, like contribute to charity and help those unable to help themselves? How will wealth give you joy and happiness?

By all means, you should visualize wealth. There is enough abundance in the world, and you have the power to attract it and use it for great things.

- **Health** - Everyone wants good health. Our thoughts can cause some health issues. For example, significant stress in your life can translate to back problems.

Some of the thinking in regards to this is the blood flow to the back area, can be disrupted, causing the small muscles to constrict, which in turn make the larger muscles overwork... causing pain.

Creating a vision board with images of how you want to feel mentally and physically, will attract opportunities into your life. In creating a health board, you need first to decide what you believe in. Everyone will have a different board.

Some boards might have pictures of vital herbs that can be used to make healthy teas or to add to their food. Others might have images of someone getting a massage with healing crystals that are said to invoke great health.

If you do not have a strong belief or get a positive, happy image in your mind from herbs or crystals, then you would omit that. Make notes of what images work for you. People exercising and healthy fruit/vegetables for instance.

Once you get your images, then it's collecting the other items for your board and start building. Start visualizing eating healthy and working out to become the best you.

- **Home** - For vision boards based on your ideal home, think of not only the exterior but the interior as well.

  Make notes of how many rooms you want. Do you want a specialty room, like a meditation room with a fish tank or objects that give you peace and tranquility?

  Visualize being in the house and walking each and every room. Thinking about how your house smells is also powerful. As you walk in your mind through the house, can you smell roses or savory herbs from your kitchen supplies?

  How does each room make you feel and how would it positively affect your family? Make the home a very happy place that you can enjoy every minute.

- **Relationships** - Vision boards for relationships are great for individuals or couples.

As an individual who wants to attract a specific type of person into your life, a vision board can give you a much clearer idea of what you are looking for in a partner. Again, everyone will have something different. You may not have much emotion around a physical type, but you might become ecstatic at attracting a loving, caring individual into your life.

For couples, a vision board can clarify what your relationship is and where you want it to grow. The vision board should express what you want from each other and the life you want to build. Include what hobbies you would both enjoy, the travel you want to incorporate as well.

A deep, meaningful connection is a beautiful thing for a couple and using a vision board can help you to find the things that will bring more passion and love to your relationship.

- **Self-care** is something many people struggle with. Depression, anxiety, and feeling of inferiority can affect anyone. Creating a vision board and visualizing happiness, feelings of total relaxation and being at peace with yourself is lovely.

Images of people meditating and doing Yoga, with positive affirmations like, "I am full of joy and radiate pure love," will make your vision board amazing.

- **Family Plus Friends** - Want to have a wonderful time? Then consider doing a family vision board. What a great rainy day activity. Before beginning this fun activity, look at where you live. What space can you use, a spare room, the basement or the garage? You will be creating a large vision board, probably made up of multiple pieces of Bristol board or brown paper for example.

Once you have decided that, hunker down with your family and start the ball rolling with lots of questions. Tell your family that there are no wrong answers and basically anything goes. Get set to learn things about your children and perhaps even your spouse-which you never knew before. Asks questions about what they want to be, want to do right now and in the future.

For example, do they want to travel, collect anything special or what they want to become in the future?

Get a large number of supplies ready and get to pasting the images of perhaps Disneyland or Australia on the vision board. Have lots of markers as well. This vision board exercise should be lots of fun...maybe even make it a pizza party as well.

When you look at your friend group, do you have some friends who share the same mindset as you? Are they reading positive books, look for documentaries that add value to their lives? Are they givers, meaning that they already want to give back to the community/world they live in or that they have talked about such things?

Gather these people for a vision board party. This is an opportunity for everyone to take a break from life, unwind and have a lot of fun.

As with your family, you'll want to make a party of it and gather up lots of supplies to help others with their boards.

Creating boards with friends will give you new insights and also strengthen your friendship. Great friends are always there for you, but sometimes life gets in the way.

Vision boards with friends is an opportunity to go back and realize how you made these great friends and how you can achieve your visions together.

Step by Step Guide to Creating Your Vision Board

We will now cover all the elements that you need to create a compelling vision board. The only limits in creating a powerful board are the ones you impose upon yourself. But you're not going to do that because you now believe that you have no limits.

Read that over again if your belief in yourself needs a good talking to. Now then, first then up, is scheduling the time for your vision board. Building one is not a twenty-minute exercise. You need anywhere from 2-5 hours over a day or two.

Find some quiet time and let your mind go over what you want in your life. Make some journal notes as to where you want to go. Once you have that, it's time to collect your supplies. You will need a piece of Bristol board, or perhaps cork board which you can easily get at Staples or Walmart for starters. You aren't limited to Bristol or cork. You can use a nice large, clean piece of cardboard if you have some around the house.

Decide where you are going to get your images from. Many people use magazines that have pictures related to what they want to achieve. If you don't have magazines, it is easy to get some from friends, a recycling depot or even Craigslist. For other images, you can use postcards or inspirational pin-on buttons.

Do you have an excellent quality color printer? If so you can grab images from the internet and print those out to trim later.

You want to choose what you know will stimulate your mind when you finish your board. Be careful with the images you choose. As you pick a picture, if you start to get a negative feeling, you have to either discard that image or take some time and work through why the image is causing negativity.

Let's look at this example. Maybe you have worked hard all your life. Yet, your bank account is always low, the apartment you live in has seen better days....and you cut out a picture of a beautiful four bedroom, two bathroom house. Suddenly as you look at the image, you feel negative. You start doubting that you can ever own a house like that.

In this case, you have two choices. You either need to discard that image and find perhaps a smaller 3 bedroom house that you totally believe can be yours or work through the negative thoughts and break down that limited feeling. You need to believe 100% that you have the power within you, to make what your vision come true.

Decide on the powerful statements/affirmations you want on the board, next to your images. You can write the affirmations used bright colored pencils or if you want the declaration attached to the image, then use the sticky note variety that comes in various "arrow," shapes.

Further tools that you will need include scissors for cutting out the images and trimming them to size. You will need to attach your pictures, so if it is on Bristol board, you will need glue.

For cork board, purchase a small box of the colored push pins to secure your images. The sky is the limit for tools used in vision board creation.

The supplies are inexpensive and if you have no issue with spending a few dollars, consider getting a rubber stamp made.

The idea would be to have a short super affirmation on a rubber stamp. You could then press it into the accompanying ink pad and apply it in one or more places on your vision board.

Let's not stop there. You just created your most powerful message. Why not apply it to as many physical spots as you can.

Spend a lot of time in the garage and have some empty wall space? Apply that message there. A hobbies room? Get a youngster to put the stamp to a Bristol board over and over again.

Kids love this stuff. Once your board is full, find a spot to hang it. Your imagination should run wild here.

The idea of creating your board is to put only images and phrases that are going to ignite your vision. In this case, you need to go with less is better.

While making a collage of images/words, you do not want it to be overwhelming to the point, your focus is taken away.

You also want to create the board with the idea of "how do I want to feel in regards to this?"

The biggest mistake people make with this is they start cutting and clipping images while forgetting the primary purpose. They get overexcited as they get pictures set and the next thing they know, they have images of Rolex watches, Porsche sports cars, and a star athlete's mansion.

Your feelings about what you want must be totally aligned with the image you glue to the board. Once you put your board together in this manner, take the time to sit back and look at it.

Look at each image and phrase. How do they speak to you? Any image or phrase that does not invoke a sense of pure excitement and feeling 100% that your vision will come true...should be removed and replaced with one that does.

Step by Step to Create Your Digital Vision Board

As with a physical vision board, you need first to decide what to focus on. When you are ready actually to start creating a digital board, then you can use Pinterest, Canva or Picmonkey.

Again you need to collect images for your digital board. Once you log-in at Pinterest, create a new board and label it for the current year. Each image that you pin to the board can be customized by using the edit button.

Looking at your board and seeing you have an image of a check for $10,000, you can write in, "I earn $10,000 a month in my home business."

This is very powerful, and actor Jim Carrey talks about how when he was broke, he wrote himself a huge check and placed it in his wallet. Every day, he took the check out and envisioned that he currently earned that much money. It came true for Jim Carrey.

Other people have taken that a step further. They get the check blown up and laminated. Then they place the check where they will see it every day. You can pin as you want under your vision board.

With Canva.com, you can use it alone or in conjunction with Pinterest. Canva is a free graphics tool, which you can use to make infographics, ebook covers and of course, vision boards.

The images you gathered for Pinterest can be uploaded to Canva. Canva has a poster template that would be perfect for vision boards. There are video tutorials on YouTube that are very good for learning how to create a vision board that will look just like one created on poster board.

Once you create and save your vision board in Canva, save and download it. You can now install that vision board as your desktop wallpaper. Also, do this on your cellphone and any other digital devices.

Would you like to use Picmonkey to create your vision board? Setup a Picmonkey account and then go to the home page. Hit the create button and choose blank canvas.

You can use a combination of Picmonkey graphics and your own uploaded images. Then hit the text tab and layer in your chosen affirmations.

Don't forget to save your work and download. Picmonkey also has a cellphone app, which can be used to create your perfect vision board.

Creating a Vision Board For Your Business- A Step by Step Guide

Vision boards for your business are essential, and you should seriously consider having more than one. Next, we will go over a step by step process of vision board success.

1. A business plan will keep you on track. If you do not have a business plan and do not want to research how to create one, there are freelance business writers who specialize in that. They will interview you and then create your plan from that.

2. Vision boards for businesses may be different depending on the size of your business. In a large scale business, it is a good idea to assemble a team to build the board.

    Each person will bring a unique vision to the creation process. It is possible that tasks for building the board will be assigned to different people, depending on that person's strength. As well, it is likely that the vision board will be much larger than the Bristol board type. In fact, the whiteboard will probably be used, and this will take up a large portion of one wall in the meeting room.

    Schedule the time needed to complete the board. To make the process completion a reward time-this would be the opportunity to have luncheon with the team.

    Assemble everyone and discuss the board as a whole.

Make sure to allow enough time that each person can point out their contribution. You want them to explain to the group why they chose the images and words. Then they should tell why those images and words moved them.

Have them explain the feelings they get when they look at their portion. Is it joy, total belief, a desire to be totally successful? Write it down in your journal, so that it can be reviewed.

3. Once you have your business plan, attach it to your vision board. Now look for images that will help you achieve success in reaching your goals.

    Ideas for this are, perhaps you need an investor for capital. Then find pictures of people or businesses that may be interested in helping your business grow and put that on the board.

    Starting out, you may be a sole proprietor. You want to have 3-5 great people working for you. Find images of where you would go to connect with people like this.

    Perhaps you need a graphic designer and are willing to try someone who just graduated from a graphics course. You could get an image of that college and put it on the board.

Build out your board with the positive images and sayings that you need to attract what you want.

4. Each business board will be different. We can use an example here just to get you started. Some businesses do well even in a recession, like those that sell coffee or chocolate.
In this example, you have one coffee shop that sells specialty coffee and dark chocolate. But you want to expand of course. On your vision board, you would put an image of what you want your 2nd coffee/chocolate store to look like. You would want an exterior image and an interior. Where do you want to expand to? Do you want to stay local or grow nationally? Find a map of the area you want to expand in and have it reduced to a size that will fit on a large board. Mark the spots where you want your 2nd, 3rd, 4th stores and more. Use some colored arrows to go beside those stores, with affirmations to make it happen. Have a goals space. Here you want to list out exactly what your expansion goals are, with a time frame to have it completed. Then write down the big "Why," under that.

Another example would be that of a real estate broker. That person would have a business vision board that would include a map of the territory they serve. Then they would put down what they want to earn, with images and affirmations that match. It would also be important for a broker to have an image of any real estate award they want to win.

Most sales organizations have a level achievement that all seller strive to reach. This is a high motivation for anyone in real estate. In life insurance, all reps are conditioned to make it to the "Million Dollar Roundtable." This is one of the highest honor they can receive.

Creating a Vision Board in Your Journal

Vision board journals are fun to create and quite portable. This means they can be viewed virtually anywhere, like a dentist office waiting room that does not allow cellphone use. Because there are already multiple pages, you can continue to build onto your vision board and layer each success with a new vision.
A vision journal requires a different type of cover than a daily journal. While daily journals might be moleskin,

your vision journal needs bright, colorful covers that create a positive attitude the moment you pick it up. There are journals available with various animals or pattern designs. If pictures of baby animals move you to feel joy, then you may want to find a journal like that. Another tip you can use is to wait before clipping out images from a magazine and get clear on what you want. A sentence may come to mind like, "I want to have a healthy body and a healthy mind to achieve my best results."

You could then reduce that sentence to one word that creates a massive pleasurable feeling. The word might be "energy," or "electric." Words move us. They can give us very pleasurable feelings. That is why poetry sparks wonderful feelings.

The word electric is powerful. You should use it often. Look back at the poem by Walt Whitman, in his 1855 "Leaves of Grass." It's called, "I Sing the Body Electric." How does that sentence make you feel right now? Energized, excited...electric like high voltage?

These are the types of words and images, you need in your vision journal, and handwriting them is also powerful.

Inside the cover, you can apply dried flowers or dried herbs that give off a very pleasing scent. You will use many of the same types of tools to create a vision journal or planner as you would a large board.

Yet in a journal, it is more likely that you will use some of the pages for doodling. This is being creative at its best.

Before beginning your vision journal, you should go through the same process of getting clear on what you want to ask the universe for. What do you want to attract into your life?

After you have glued in your images and written your affirmations or powerful statements, set aside some blank pages to come and doodle in. When you doodle, first take a few deep breaths and clear your mind and then just begin. Let it flow and see where your creativity takes you.

Another section of pages can be used for a YES or NO set of columns. You have your goals, and in this section, you can point form what you will do and what you won't do. So if someone offers you an opportunity because you have put your intentions out to the universe, you can come back to the journal and see if that offer fits the YES or NO column. This is perfect for weeding out the offers that do not move you forward.

The back page of a vision journal is a great place to list out the books you will read to improve your mind. You can make a list and beside it, write a brief statement of what this book means to you. How will it make you feel? How will this help you achieve your goals? Only pick books you get a powerful mental image and feeling from.

You can do your vision journal as a collage, layering one image over the border of another. Yet another way to do it is like a mind map. Put a large image central on the page and use smaller images to branch out from the larger. Either way needs to get your imagination and law of attraction moving forward.

Take the 10-Day Vision Board Challenge! –

https://kimberlythemillionaire.thinkific.com/courses/10-day-visioning-board-challenge

How To Start a Vision Board Party

Hosting parties can be time-consuming but very rewarding. Many professional scrapbookers, hold parties to teach people how to create their own cards, photograph albums, and even vision boards. Scrapbooking and vision boards can go hand in hand because of the tools used.

No you don't have to be a professional scrapbooker to hold a vision board party, however. A vision board party is merely a way to get people together who have a very common goal and then learn from each other.

While your guests should have a common goal, the idea is to have a wide variety of people. Try to get a group of people from different work areas, ages, different hobbies and yes having an introvert or two included is always a good idea. The mindset of introverts and extroverts is quite different, but each group can bring something to the table.

While everyone should bring a small staple of their own supplies and their own bare board, as the host you should stock up on a wide assortment of magazines, old books with pictures and lots of sticky type note pads of varying shapes and sizes. Have some extra scissors, glue and such, since there is always going to be one or two people who forgot their supplies or were running late and didn't have time to grab stuff.

Have everyone introduce themselves and give a rundown on why they wanted to attend the party. What do they want to achieve? If you have someone at the party who has created and used a vision board with great success, make sure to give them ample time to tell their story.

Many people are uncomfortable when attending parties and take a while to settle in. You should make sure to on your invitations to tell people this party is scheduled for 6 pm to midnight or something similar. This gives you time to warm people up.

Perhaps a quick party game to get everyone loose and laughing. While you will be serving some food and beverages, it best to stick with water/soft drinks to start the evening.

A glass of wine added to the evening is fine. You want your guests clear-headed to give their best during the creation of their vision boards and not have any issues with people getting home safely afterward.

Stay away from messy foods, like a big pot of spaghetti or your famous hot wings. K your work area clean, and people trying to get ahead of the game by flipping through magazines with barbeque sauce on their fingers will create a mess. Go with a variety of salads, mixed cheese or even veggies and dip.

You put together an excellent list of people and hopefully you have some understanding of what music you want to play softly in the background. It cannot be distracting and pulling attention away from the creation of the vision boards.

Everyone should be encouraged to share their boards during the creation and afterward. Seeing another person's board can be extremely helpful in understanding how to get the juices flowing and start attracting what you want in your life.

It's very likely that some people will gather totally new ideas and either add to their boards straight away or create a brand new one that serves them better.

Do You Like Coaching? Start a Vision Board Workshop

One pathway to success is being a coach. Many people struggle in different areas. They need help and of course, are willing to pay for it. Many people will hire a coach, achieve success and then hire a more advanced coach to take them to the next level. Lifestyle coaching is enormous and being a Vision Board coach is one way of adding to your income stream.

Doing a webinar on vision boards might be the first thing to come to your mind. To be really successful at it, then consider doing your workshops in person. You've built a vision board.

You understand the attraction process because your dreams came true due to what you visualized. Others need your passion and your experience.

It's not necessary to have some certification in coaching. You have real-life experience, and people will know, like and trust you, when they see you in person and hear the passion in your voice.

You need to spend quality time planning out your workshop. The first item of business is coming up with a title for your workshop.

Grab a clean notebook and come up with ten great titles. Take your time working through the title ideas, crossing out ideas until you are left with the best. Decide how long your workshop will be.

Consider, whether or not you have spoken before in front of people. If you have not done a lot, then practice in front of a family member or friend and get feedback. Get them to rate you for voice quality, passion and the ability to get your message across.

You do not have to be perfect, but you do need to be able to speak for long periods and maintain your flow. If you have not spoken in front of a crowd, then keep your first workshop small. Decide how many people you feel could be in the room and you would have them spellbound.

You will need to rent some space in your area. Many venues can accommodate you.

Make a list and start calling to find out times available and what they charge. From that, you can decide how much you need to charge per person for your workshop, to pay the room fee and make a profit.

Profit! Absolutely you want to make a good profit, and in this, you also need to decide how you will allow people to pay for the workshop. You need payment upfront and decide about cancellation times and if you will charge a fee for last minute cancellation.

You are booking a room that has to be paid for, so make it known to your potential clients that they have to be serious about attending. How they pay is really up to you.

Since they are paying in advance-a mobile phone with a credit card swipe won't work. It will have to be

PayPal, a credit card merchant account if you have one or a money order.

You will also need to find out how long you can have the room for and write that down. Once you get it narrowed down and make your decision, go ahead and book the room. Don't wait. You need to go with the idea that there is no turning back and you are going to visualize a supremely successful workshop.

Work out where you will connect with potential clients. If you are on LinkedIn with a good number of connections, you could start posting in there.

Create a Facebook fan page, use your Twitter or do some YouTube videos.

Creating a landing page and explaining your workshop, with an opt-in box, is also another possibility. Think about the people whose email address you already have or can get with little effort.

You will want to set up an email system for several reasons. Aweber is the best one to use, but if you are on a tight budget, there are free options. In getting email addresses, you will be manually importing the data or the address will be added when someone opts in.

You will want to put together an information sheet that details the workshop, what people should expect and what you will be bringing to the conversation. You could use this sheet to tell people what supplies they need to bring and what the day or days will include, depending on how long you make your course.

Sharing your success story and the success stories of others will help to sell this workshop. When you have succeeded in building and using a vision board, it is a great idea to teach your family and your close friends to do the same. They can be your first unpaid clients and telling how they succeeded, gives you credibility. This sheet can be made into a PDF and delivered by email.

The final part of your workshop is coming up with some worksheets that you can pass out, and people can fill in during the start of the course.

You need to build an outline of what you are teaching and have a fill in the blanks worksheet to help people access the internal resources that they have but may never have used.

Finally, it is a great idea to have a feedback sheet for people to complete at the end. Use the feedback to improve your workshops.

Vision Board Tools and Apps

In this section, we will cover apps that can be used to create vision boards. You will need to explore each app and see which one is right for you. There are both free and paid apps, some of which are based on subliminal messages.

When looking at apps, you may search for others not listed here. Just be aware of what the app will do and that it may include ads, which of course you do not want to have in a vision board app.

Subliminal messages can enter the brain and over-write the negative messages that may have been stored there for years.

Always read any caution messages regarding subliminals, to ensure safe usage. As well, the information in this section will be covering apps that are IOS only or useable in IOS/Android. Let's start with an IOS that resembles the physical corkboard.

Corkulous Pro is an IOS only, and when the app is open, you are shown a corkboard. You can have one corkboard or multiple corkboards as this app supports sub-corkboards. Use the corkboard to place your images, written text, tasks, and even emojis.

This app allows you to share using Dropbox so you can send copies of your vision board to workmates or friends. The app has a free and a paid version, however, the paid version is under $10 at the time of this eBook.

Subliminal Vision Boards - This app is based directly on the LOA-Law of Attraction principle and uses animated features.

You can create unlimited boards, and they are multi-sensory.

Once your boards are created, the app will have you watching the screen, while the images and text you created are rapid fired into your brain. This allows them to bypass your conscious brain and not give it a chance to have a doubt about what you have written.

The images and text are picked up by your subconscious mind which believes what you tell it and will start to work immediately on what you really want in your life.

You can create your own affirmations or use some of the 100 pre-written affirmations. Add in some relaxing music and then put on the headphones to help get the best visual/auditory experience.

On the google play store, it sells for $6.49. There are several apps with similar names. At this point in time, SVB is on the top.

Vision Board by Astraport - This is available in Google Play or the Apple App store. This app has its own symbols for putting together your vision board, or you can import your own.

There are 311 wish symbols that can be taken from 18 different categories, so you can start accomplishing the things you've only been dreaming about for so long, like getting rid of any extra weight you may be carrying, or finally manifest the money you deserve. It's packed with 118 ready for your affirmations, to reprogram your mind for success. It has 7 done for you templates in popular themes, or you can create your own.

To make sure you succeed at creating a perfect vision board on your phone, they have included an excellent tutorial. However, try not to watch the tutorial on your phone and then create your vision board. There are elements to the control panel that are hard to see on a cellphone, so watch the tutorial on YouTube.

Open your screen fully and then open the app on your phone. You can simply follow along and pause the video as needed. It is very easy to create a fantastic vision board this way with Astraport Pro.

They give you a 7-day free trial. After that, if you love it and you will, then you can choose from a monthly or yearly subscription. Here is the YouTube link.
https://youtu.be/L6MFtWx4FjA

VISUAPP is a free tool on the google play store. It has great reviews. This app allows you to search for your vision or dream on your current browser and then share it directly to the app. You can take pictures of what you visualize as yours, such a nice car or a hidden cottage by a peaceful river. Those pictures can then be transferred into the app, where you will then add the affirmations.

VISUAPP is big on Feng-Shu. It has 8 Feng-Shu boards, on topics like money, relationships, career, and creativity. When you create your board, you can put it on single mode or have it set-up as a slide show. There are many cool options inside this free app.

VisionBoard.cc is a free online software. You can set up an account and then start creating your board online. Your board can become your homepage with this software. Your images can come directly from what you already have on your computer or search and upload to your board and then put your text affirmations on the board. There is a community of people who share the visions you have. You can join the community and learn new ways to visualize your most desired dreams.

Simple Vision Board – This is another online software that you can access on your computer. It's free, and it helps you create your very own Vision Board easy and fast. This makes it ideal when trying to create your first draft, or if you want to create different Vision Boards, one for each area of your life.

Bonus Section: How to Vision Board For Your Children

Vision boards for children are more important today than ever before. Children are bombarded with negativity and are needing to make serious choices at a much younger age.

Feeding your children's minds with healthy positive images and statements will do more for them in the long run, than enrolling them in extra math classes on the weekend.

With vision boards, they can learn how to be positive about themselves, mind and body. As well, they can learn to contribute to others and get joy from helping others.

Spending time creating a vision board with your child will also be very rewarding for you. It's a chance to see how your child views their world at the moment and help them make adjustments to serve them better.

Bristol board is excellent for vision boards and in the case of your child, you may want to connect more than one, to give them ample room to work on building their vision for the days to come. You could even get an extra-large piece of brown parcel paper and make a five-foot-long vision board that will adorn one wall of their bedroom.

Spend some time with your child getting the supplies together. Crayons, colored pencils, images from magazines or children's books for starters. Since this is a children's board, you may even want to gather some ribbons to really color up the borders and make the vision board pop.

After all the supplies are gathered, it's time for a little party. Gather up some favorite snacks and then sit down with the child and talk about what the purpose of the board is. Explain that it is a way to express love. Ask them questions about who do they love? Family, friends, pets and even people they don't know but have a positive feeling about. They can choose pictures of those they express love about.

Next talk about what they love to do and what they would like to do over the next three, six and twelve months. What excites them? Ask if they have any dreams of becoming a vet or growing up to be an artist? Talk about what your child is passionate about.

When you have all the elements you need, then start putting the board together. Let your child do most of the creating. This is a coaching opportunity for you.

Ask them, "Why did you put that picture there? How does this picture make you feel? What colors would you like to write in beside that picture? When you choose that color, how does it make you feel?"

The vision board for kids is also an excellent place for them to learn how to create goals for themselves. Teach them how to set goals that are appropriate for their age and also to put time for reaching the goal as well as, the proper rewards for setting and meeting goals.

Make the goals specific. For example, if the child usually gets a C in reading, then have them set a goal of reading time to improve, and what grade they want to achieve next.

As with adults, the child should track their progress, so going to the store and picking up some stickers that are visually appealing to your child is a good idea.

Conclusion

We have gone over all the essentials of vision boards. As well, it is likely that you now see how vision boards are a must for everyone and every business. The next step is taking action, and the best way to do that is close this ebook and take at least one action right away before doing anything else.

It could be making a list of supplies, outlining goals or feelings of gratitude. Action with passion will be the first stepping stone to creating the life you have always desired.

To help with your vision boards, a vision board challenge has been created. The 10 Day Vision Board Challenge will be fun and rewarding. Make sure not to skip over any elements of the challenge and reap the success you deserve.

Take the 10-Day Vision Board Challenge! –
https://kimberlythemillionaire.thinkific.com/courses/10-day-
visioning-board-challenge

Bonus Idea!!!

Take things to the next level by creating your OWN line of vision journals! The process is so simple and easy, you will be flowing with ideas and producing tons of journals in no time!

Build your own passive income stream with this easy-to-do model. Just go to:

http://kimberlythemillionaire.thinkific.com/courses/passive-publishing-income

and get started TODAY!